AUTHOR'

Charlottesville, Virginia is a good place to start. That is where I was born in 1921 and where I am now writing this story in 2001. Charlottesville is about 115 miles south of Washington, D.C. and about 70 miles west of Richmond, Virginia. We are what you might call a "stone's throw" from the foothills of the Blue Ridge Mountains. From other places that I have seen, Charlottesville seemed to be a great place to grow up.

In my early childhood, I didn't know about many other cities, so I couldn't really judge. During those pre-school years, my sister and brother and I would often gather in our mothers' warm kitchen on cold, cloudy, wintry days. We would bring our crayons and coloring books, jigsaw puzzles and the color comics from the last Sunday's *Washington Post* (Then I believe it was called the *Washington Herald*). No big deal, these were just everyday things we thought everyone did.

It was during one of those kitchen days in 1927 that I learned about Charles Lindbergh. In 1927, there was no television and very few people had radios. All the information we ever received was from nosey women, rumor mongers, school teachers, preachers and the local newspaper, any one of which was as reliable as the other. Mother had a paper with many pictures of Lindbergh and his plane "The Spirit of St. Louis." The story told of his solo flight from the United States over the Atlantic Ocean to Paris, France. I was only six years old when Mother showed me the pictures and explained what a hero was. She said he was the very first man to ever do such a thing. Well, that was the first hero I had ever known. Until that day, I didn't even know what the word meant.

To put things in perspective of the times, that era was well before all of the mass media coverage that we are accustomed to today. News items took a long time to circulate around the world. It actually wasn't so different from the time that Abraham Lincoln was shot in Washington, D.C. It took a week for the people in California to hear about it! Times have changed a bit.

Thomas M. Behrendt
Author

PACIFIC DIARY

From Charlottesville to Kyoto
1927 - 1945

By
Thomas M. Behrendt

ISBN: 1-885354-09-6

This edition published by arrangement with Honoribus Press.

First Printing: May, 2001

Printed in the United States of America
Altman Printing Co., Inc.
Spartanburg, South Carolina

DEDICATION

This book is dedicated to my girls! All of my Behrendt girls. To my wife Doris for all the times she just let me be alone, when my grey matter was at it's best and the juices were flowing . . . alone to persue my thoughts. She was also my "Webster" whenever I couldn't find a word in his dictionary. This book is dedicated to my three daughters: Terry Hamlett, a legal assistant with a group of lawyers on Court Square here in Charlottesville; Susan Gibson, a Registered Nurse at the University of Virginia Hospital; and JoAnne Kice, who operates her own Interior Design Company, also here in Charlottesville. When it comes to those three, I count my blessings. I particularly want to thank JoAnne for all the work she did and all the time she spent on the much appreciated editing and the transferring of the entire text from the typewritten original to the new computer. I love you all so very much.

– Thomas M. Behrendt
May, 2001

Cadet Thomas M. Behrendt, Augusta Military Academy, 1940.

ACKNOWLEDGEMENTS

It would be virtually impossible to name every person on this planet that may have had some part in enabling me to write this book. Where do I start? I think the really first person who unknowingly set me in that direction was my mother. Yep, she's the one. Blame her. She was a wonderful mother who gave me my first typewriter as a Christmas present when I was ten years old. Maybe she thought I would amount to something as a writer if I started early enough. I was born in 1921 and I got the typewriter in 1931. This is now 2001 and I just finished my first book. WOW! If she'd given me the typewriter any later I might have done this from a wheelchair. My mother waited as long as she could and finally gave up and passed away at age 97. I no longer have that first typewriter but I still have the wonderful memories that came with it. My favorite brother-in-law and he happens to be the only one, (if I had others, he would still be my favorite) and I were discussing how little our children know about us before we became their father. We suddenly realized the time had come to write a book! He is Dr. Charles Gleason, a retired pediatrician. He also gets the blame. (I know I'll get some of the blame when he does his book!) I would also like to thank Mrs. McCue for that year in her typing class at Lane High School in 1935. And, I would like to thank the rest of the world just for being there! It's the people you meet and the places you go that encourage you to put it on paper for others to enjoy. Writing is the art of teaching and entertaining and I like to think that in this book, I have done a little of both. A special thanks to Colonel Ed. Y. Hall of Honoribus Press for his assistance in producing *Pacific Diary*.

Augusta Military Academy

TABLE OF CONTENTS

Author's Note

Dedication

Acknowledgements

Doris Behrendt – Wife of Author
Administrative Secretary Rock Hill Academy – 1964-1988
Charlottesville, Virginia

Chapter 1

GROWING UP

All Americans should know their history. All history is important, but the history of America is so unique. Today, I suspect the people in France know more about the feats of Lindbergh than do many Americans. Lindbergh was well known around the world as well as being a national hero. In my mind, any man that would get in a little single plane alone, with only a pocket full of Hershey Bars and an instrument panel that didn't work most of the time and fly over the ocean at night, has got to be either a hero or nuts! I think he was the former.

Later on in life, I discovered another American hero: John Wayne. "The Duke." The epitome of the Hollywood Cowboy and a great western hero. (Of course, as a youngster who saw his first western movie at the local Lafayette Theatre in the mid thirties, the hero's of the west in those days were Buck Jones, Ken Maynard, Charles Starrett, Hoot Gibson, Tim McCoy, Johnny MacBrown, Bob Steele, Tom Tyler and a few others). John Wayne was, as the title of one of his western movies suggests, *"Tall in the Saddle."* He had great acting ability, good looks, and the staying power of the best in Hollywood for almost fifty years.

Back to growing up in Charlottesville. As was the case with many young men of that era, I had daily classes at Lane High School, delivered newspapers (The Richmond News Leader), listened to big band music and nearly every Saturday afternoon I could be found at the Lafayette Theatre.

I was beginning to find out that there were many advantages to living in Charlottesville, like the University of Virginia. So many activities that we just took for granted. UVA had one of the best boxing teams in the nation and it was seldom that any of the boys at Lane High ever missed a match. UVA football at Lambeth Field and later at the new Scott Stadium. Numerous places for the students to gather and occasionally enjoy a cool German Lager, and many of us at Lane High School made ourselves a big part of that scene. Hanging out with the students not only made us feel like adults, but it was also very easy to buy pitchers of beer, even in our early teens.

The greatest memory for me was the arrival of the big bands! All of the big name bands came to town in the 30's, 40's, and 50's to play for the dances and concerts at UVA. Tommy Dorsey, Benny Goodman, Louis Armstrong, Duke Ellington, Count Basie, Lionell Hampton, Woody Herman, Les Brown, Tex Benekie and the Glenn Miller Orchestra, Charlie Barnet, Sammy Kaye and a host of others. One of the first to appear in Memorial Gymnasium in 1930 was Guy Lombardo. The final two were Charlie Barnet and Ralph Marterie in 1960. Apparently, the big band era had ended.

My high school years in Charlottesville were very adventurous with many pretty girls and parties every Friday and Saturday night. There were nights of drinking beer with my friend Harry Linton at Fry Spring's Beach Club or at the Cavalier on the University of Virginia "Corner." Both places had juke boxes that played continually into the night and in the mid thirties the songs or tunes that we heard over and over were Tommy Dorsey's "Marie" and "Song of India." They were undoubtedly two of the biggest radio hits of that era and a number one seller on the old "78" records. I remember when we had dates and would go to a dance at Fry Spring's and dance to bands named the "Cavaliers" or the "Virginians" and sometimes Hartwell Clark and his band. The big thrill for us in those mid-teen years was going to Memorial Gym at the University of Virginia when the big bands were in town. Since there was no air conditioning in those days it was imperative that the gym's big side doors were kept open to circulate the air in all kind of weather. The University dance committee would let us high school boys guard the doors. There was no drinking allowed in the gym so whenever the students and their dates would go out for a "nip," we would hand them a ticket to use in order to regain admittance. It was a great thrill for me standing on the same floor right next to the biggest bands in the nation. In the 1930's there was no television so this was the first time many of us had seen anything like this. A major event in our young lives.

Cadets on Parade
Augusta Military Academy

Cadet Tom Behrendt
Augusta Military Academy – 1938

Chapter 2

AUGUSTA MILITARY ACADEMY

Unfortunately, these fun times outside of school were taking a toll on my grades. My parents got stricter with me and let me use the car only one night a week. My dear mother convinced me that I would love attending Augusta Military Academy in nearby Fort Defiance, Virginia in the beautiful Shenandoah Valley. She was right (although "liked" is more appropriate than "loved.") In any case I entered AMA in the fall of 1937 and graduated in the summer of 1940. AMA was a good school and I made many friends, some of which I still hear from almost every year. My father taught me about honesty and the importance of keeping my word, but it was AMA that taught me to love my country. I played the National Anthem on my trombone in the band every night for three years, and it is permanently embedded in my soul. Through some ROTC classes we learned about the ways of war, including how to take a machine gun apart and then put it back together again in the dark. I think most boys enjoyed taking things apart to see if they could reassemble it in the proper order. We also marched a lot. I liked close order drill and actually became very proficient at it. There was something about the beat – the rhythm of marching feet that made you want to strut your stuff! When there was a good marching band with a stepped-up cadence, they just couldn't hold me down!

AMA was a fun place to learn all of these skills. You couldn't learn them in public school, which is a shame. I can usually tell after a relatively short time whether or not a new acquaintance has had any form of military training, even after all of those years. I believe it makes for a better person. There's something about a man's character, his distinguishing qualities and moral strength that sets him apart from the rest.

Of course all of these fine thoughts about the many advantages of military training came later in my life. As young cadets at AMA, many of us were looking for ways to bend the rules. One event I remember vividly happened during a delightful spring evening. Several of us had just returned to our barracks after dinner in the mess hall and were enjoying the "free" time before study hall. As usual, a small group of friends gathered out on the stoop in the warm early evening hours of mid-May, waiting for the call to "hit the books." This was during the golden years of radio and we were discussing the very popular Fred Allen Show. There was a weekly feature in which the announcer exclaimed "It's Town Hall Tonight!" which was immediately followed by a musical rendition that could easily be sung or hummed without the use of words. Well, somebody (I can't imagine who) thought it would be fun to yell out "It's Town Hall Tonight" and sing the famous theme in the middle of study hall. It was just too fine a day not to do something, and we were young and eager to make our presence known. Perhaps this was not the best way to do it, but at the time it was perfect!

Study hall was held each week-night in the "Big Room" of the Academic Building at the far end of campus. A scattering of about 30 or 40 cadets were studying at their desks as the very new and very young Lieutenant Twombly, the officer in charge on that particular night, was quietly reading at a desk on a stage at the front of the room. There were probably six of us in cahoots in this endeavor, and at a prearranged silent signal the exclamation began: "It's Town Hall Tonight!" immediately followed by the musical theme that we all knew so well. The only problem was that the other five guys (the traitors) didn't say a word! They had chickened out at the last minute, leaving me to my solo, and I sang the whole damn thing, loud and clear. My desk was on the right side of the room, about two-thirds down from the front. When I began to yell, Lieutenant Twombly sprung out of his chair and looked like he was in complete shock as he bolted down the aisle to my desk. By then I had risen to my feet, still singing. He stopped about six inches from my face and yelled, "Behrendt, have you lost your mind?" Before I could think of a good answer, he ushered me out of the building to the outside front steps and proceeded to give me a tongue-lashing. Before sending me back to my desk he said he was going to report me to Major Roller (the head of the school). The Lieutenant left and as I headed back to my desk I noted that not one in all of the cadets in that room had made a sound, not one sound (including my friends the traitors). After a time, Lieutenant Twombly returned and ordered me in front of the other cadets to report to the Commandant's Office. You don't think at a time like that, you just do it.

Well, good luck was with me that night. Major Roller was at a Kiwanas meeting in Staunton and Major Herbert Deane was holding down the fort. There was always a senior faculty advisor on duty in the barracks. Some nights it was Major Roller himself, but thank God, on this night it was Major Deane. The nervous, shaking Lieutenant Twombly had of course reported the incident to the Major, who in turn wanted to hear my version.

I didn't know anything other than to tell the whole truth, so I recanted the entire story to him. He wanted to know who the other five cadets were so I told him. He said that what I had done was wrong, but he was proud of me because I didn't let the others down and did exactly what I said I would do. Believe it or not, I was let off, scot free, while the five others received a royal chewing-out, demerits, and late night tours followed by a week of shoveling coal!

I suppose the purpose in recalling my time at AMA is really two fold. One is to bring back some of the fond memories of my young care-free days, but more importantly to reminisce about the

many fine teachers there. The values we learn will live with us for-
ever, and on this particular occasion I was again reminded of the
absolute necessity of keeping my word. (And the really satisfying
part is that the other five men had to learn that lesson the hard way).

Military schools can be very beneficial to young teenagers particularly those who may need help in determining the best direction
to take in order to achieve a productive and happy life. Many young
men don't have personal goals because often they are defeated
before they begin. Many say they would rather just sit around and
wait to see what's going to happen. Occasionally crazy things will
happen that help us to decide just what direction to take.

One night in October of 1938 when we were all in our rooms
during a break from study hall, a cadet ran into our room and
shouted: "Turn on your radio! Men from Mars have landed in
New Jersey!" "Yeah, yeah, yeah" I said, "and AMA is going to
close and we are all going home." "No, it's really on the radio!
Turn it on and you can hear it for yourself!" he exclaimed. Well,
naturally we did turn on the radio and damn if it didn't sound
like the real thing. We didn't know whether to believe it or not.
It was broadcast in such a way that it appeared to really be hap-
pening. The next thing I knew everybody in barracks had their
radio on as the cadets were running from room to room, check-
ing it out. Some of the boys from New Jersey had requested to
use the phone in the Officer of the Day's office to call home to
see if everything was all right. Many of us suspected that it had
to be fiction, and of course it turned out to be a dramatic, realis-
tic radio network presentation. Orson Wells had written, produced, directed and acted in this great production and aired it in
such a way that it scared much of the nation to death. It was
called "War of the Worlds." We all listened to it until the very
end, just to make sure that it was indeed a hoax. The next day the
mess hall was buzzing with chatter about the event. Some of the
guys knew for sure what they now wanted to become: a professor
in the studies of outer space; a producer of radio programs; some
even wanted to be astronauts.

Unfortunately those memorable days in beautiful Augusta
County would soon come to an end. Hitler was on a rampage in

Europe and there was talk even then of the United States becoming involved. I then realized that what I had learned in those ROTC classes could prove to be very beneficial in the months ahead.

The Colors

Graduates of Augusta Military Academy in Fort Defiance, Virginia in 1940. Arthur Mitchell (left) of Greenwood, Virginia and Tom Behrendt of Charlottesville, on their way to California in the summer of 1941.

Chapter 3

YOU'RE IN THE ARMY NOW!

After my graduation from AMA, I moved back to Charlottesville and enrolled in the University of Virginia. A year later I accepted a position with Peoples Bank and was there when the Japanese attacked Pearl Harbor on December 7th, 1941.

Two of my good friends at AMA also lived in Charlottesville. Hope ("Booty") Gleason worked for H.M. Gleason Company and Bobby Faulconer worked for Faulconer Construction Company. We all quit our jobs and volunteered our services to the United States Army on October 1, 1942. Booty went into the Air Corps, Bobby into the Field Artillery, and I ended up in the Signal Corps, and we all went off in different directions.

The Army sent me to Fort Monmouth (actually Sea Girt) New Jersey for basic training. Sea Girt was something. Specifically it was Camp Wood in Sea Girt. It was on the Jersey Shore, and we lived in tents next to the ocean which proved to be quite chilly at night. We did have kerosene heaters but in spite of that I think we all kept our socks on in bed at night.

One morning after breakfast the camp officer in charge ordered our group to stand in formation out in front of one of the tents. The first thing he said was "Has anybody in this group been to a military school?" I raised my hand. Apparently I was the only one. He said, "Get out here!" I immediately broke rank and took the position in front of the men. After asking my name the officer told me that I would be in charge of this group while in Camp Wood. I would march them to the Mess Hall three times each day and to classes in between. And most important: I would teach them Close Order Drill! Well I knew right then that this was going to be an enjoyable place. Every afternoon for almost two hours, we got to "play" - teaching the guys how to enjoy the thrill of marching. The most wonderful surprise came after a few days when they did begin to like it. Those guys were good! One of them actually told me that it was hard not to keep in step when I was doing the drilling. These guys were proud of what they were doing and I was certainly proud of them. Life is fun when it goes like that.

A short time before going into the service, I remember see-ing a movie in the Paramount Theatre in Charlottesville about the Marine Corps. It was a new, beautifully photographed film that featured the expertise of Tyrone Power and his drill team as they performed various maneuvers that no other unit had ever tried. As the platoon marched down the field, he would give orders to each squad to perform individually as they would go off in dif-ferent directions. Then on his command, each squad would reverse its direction and return to the original formation without missing a beat. This looked really sharp.

When my guys were out on the drill field one after-noon, I remembered that film. My unit was one platoon, the same size as the one in the movie and it had the usual three squads. So, what the hell, let's give it a shot. I told the men what we were going to do. I was so pleased when without exception they all said "We can do that!" Those men were not profession-al soldiers, but rather regular guys from civilian life who just wanted to be a part of what we all were trying to accomplish. We marched our unit over to the far side of the field. I wanted to get our guys away from the other groups and particularly away from the permanent officers of the camp that may have possibly

Dave Graves and Tom Behrendt on KP duty during Basic Training
in Sea Girt, New Jersey in 1942.

wanted to interfere. We wanted to get this right before we performed in front of the others. We drilled and we drilled. We were looking good. When a guy made a mistake he would apologize to the others and would invariably say "Okay, I've got it - let's do it again!" One couldn't wish for more enthusiasm than that. It wasn't long before we were proudly performing in view of the entire camp. We obviously made a big hit with the cadre at Camp Wood. So much so that I was ordered to appear before the Commandant. Oh God – what have I done now? What a surprise – they wanted me to stay there for the duration and teach all the new recruits the art of close order drill. I have always wondered if I made the right decision when I told them "thanks but no thanks." At the time I wanted to stay with my new friends and see some of the world. War is a great adventure and staying in Sea Girt would be missing all the "fun." When I've told that story to people they often say that I must have been crazy. Fortunately, I'll never know.

After our basic training was completed at Camp Wood, the Army sent us to Fort Monmouth proper, just a few miles up the road for our specialized schooling in the particular field to which we had been assigned. Our group had been designated to become cryptographers and operators of the army's new highly secret code machines.

I later found out from my father that I had been thoroughly checked out by the War Department. While we were marching around at Sea Girt, the Federal government had FBI agents in Charlottesville interviewing our neighbors, my boss and other employees at the bank, teachers at Lane High School and the Commandant at Augusta Military Academy. I must have passed with flying colors because there I was.

The code machines had a standard typewriter keyboard, and I was so grateful to my teacher Mrs. McCue for that one year of typing class at Lane High School. I think I must have benefited more from that one class than I did from any other. It was as important to my future then as the computer is to people today.

After several weeks of intensive training, we were all sent to Washington, D.C. and assigned to the message center in the

Pentagon. This was the first step in our new great adventure. While in Washington, we lived on a per diem from the Army. We lived wherever we could find a place and either ate in restaurants or in a girlfriend's apartment.

Four of us rented the space in the attic of a woman's home in Clarendon, Virginia. We walked a block to the bus stop and rode it right to the door of the Pentagon. Frequently, whenever we weren't working the night shift, several of us would go into downtown Washington to a movie or visit some of the clubs. What a great experience! For a young man in uniform during World War II, Washington was the place to be! One night one of my Clarendon roommates and I went to the Warner Brothers Earl Theatre (I believe it's simply called the Warner Theatre now). We saw the original showing of *Casablanca* with Humphrey Bogart and Ingrid Bergman. This was December, 1942 and I think the admission was about 65 cents. After the movie, a group of girls approached us and started a conversation in the lobby as we were leaving the theatre. One of the girls said we looked hungry and invited us to her place for a late night snack. Well, well, well, what's a man to do? As luck would have it, I was hungry. We got an early start making new friends in our nation's capitol. We were only doing our duty towards the war effort.

After several happy months in "Camelot" I was put in charge of a platoon of other code men as we prepared to depart for California. We were assigned to a plush Pullman Car attached to a civilian train traveling from Baltimore to Chicago and then on to San Francisco. I couldn't believe my luck. There were about 20 Privates in a private Pullman Car with a Pullman Porter – and I was in charge! We just had a ball.

On one occasion the train had stopped at a small town in the Midwest. The main street ran along the train track about 50 yards away. One of my guys spotted a liquor store and with encouragement from the others, decided to make a dash for it. The porter raised the platform and lowered the steps and off he went. He yelled back to me "tell them to wait, I'll be right back!" I don't know what we would have done if the train had taken off while he was still in the store. But as luck would have it, he came out of the store waving the bottle and running full speed back to the train. We all cheered for him and as you might imagine, I was particularly pleased to have him back on board.

That train went only as far as Chicago. The plan had been for our Pullman Car to be decoupled from our Baltimore train and then recoupled to the train leaving Chicago and heading to the West Coast. Our train was late, however, and the other train had already gone. That was at about 7am and another train wasn't leaving until 7pm. That meant we had the whole day in Chicago - a dream come true! We checked our barracks bags and rifles at the Station, grabbed a cab and headed for State Street. We went to restaurants and clubs from one end of town to the other, and were even entertained by Charlie Spivak and his orchestra at the beautiful Chicago Theatre. After that wonderful day of sightseeing, eating and drinking and making friends, we were all ready to return to our Pullman Car and prepare for our long trip to the West Coast.

It is three times further from Chicago to San Francisco than it is from Baltimore to Chicago, so we had quite a trip in front of us. Some of the guys had never been more than a few miles away from home. A fellow named Jim McNeely from South Philadelphia spotted a herd of cattle from the train window and wondered what they were – he had only seen them in cowboy movies! The same reaction came from almost the entire group when we saw a herd of buffalo.

Traveling across the country with those Yankee "homebodies" was quite a revealing experience for me. I didn't know how lucky I was to have experienced at least some travel and to know a bit about other places. Most of these guys had never been anywhere. I felt like a cross-country tour guide showing the big country to my appreciative group of foreigners! This was the big chance for all of us to see the world, or at least part of it. This was a true travel experience like none other.

Our cross-country trip on the rails finally came to an end in Pittsburgh – California that is. This Pittsburgh was a small town forty miles northeast of San Francisco in the San Pablo Bay. This was a disembark center for the American troops about to leave the country. There we got shots and more shots, new uniforms, steel helmets and all sorts of general information about how to conduct ourselves outside the United States.

After a few days in beautiful Pittsburgh, thousands of us boarded this God-forsaken freighter and slowly sailed through the San Pablo Bay, past Alcatraz, under the Golden Gate Bridge and out to the Pacific Ocean. They didn't tell us exactly where we were going until we were half way across the ocean. Next stop: Brisbane, Australia!

This trip was the worst experience of my life. They had us stacked five high on smelly stretched canvas down in a dark hole for four hellish weeks. Prisoners in Alcatraz lived under better conditions. Thank God we all made it to Australia – I'd still be there today if I had to return in that boat.

U.S. Army Photo

The Pentagon

Inspections

Basic Training

Pvt. Thomas M. Behrendt

Photo taken in Charlottesville just a few weeks after joining the Army in October, 1942.

Tom Behrendt with friend Hope "Booty" Gleason in Charlottesville in October, 1942.

The original Behrendt family in Charlottesville, Virginia in 1942.

From the left, brother Bill, then my mother, Lee Michie Behrendt, then in front center is sister Betz Gleason, then dad, T.B. Behrendt and then, yours truly, T.M.B.

Can you imagine these guys decoding secret messages? It's a wonder we won the war! My group of Signal Corps trainees at Sea Girt, NJ in the fall and winter 1942-43.

Chapter 4

AUSTRALIA

In contrast to those last four weeks, the happiest day of my entire life was about to happen. When they announced over the ship's public address system that we would be landing at Brisbane in a few hours, I was just ecstatic. It was going to be a new life for me – I can't adequately describe my feelings at that moment and for the rest of that day. Then, setting foot on the beautiful continent of Australia, I realized just how precious life can be. After the terrifying month on that ungodly freighter, I believe I can say I know what it feels like when a falsely accused prisoner is given a reprieve by the Governor: I'm free, I get to live again! I promise to be a model citizen. I will never do anything that is stupid – like getting back on that damn boat! I was ready to spend the rest of my life in Australia and we had only been there ten minutes.

Now was the time to explore Australia. Brisbane, the capital of Queensland, had a population of approximately 800,000 people. We set up tents at the local race-track where we were able to use the public rest rooms as our very own. (Believe me, anything was a luxury now). Shortly after arriving we met some very nice people, including a lady who invited me to have dinner with her in her home. The hospitality was beyond the call of duty. The meal was great and I particularly remember the delicious red tomatoes. After my recent experience, that meal was heaven.

I really didn't want to leave Brisbane but the time had come for us to move on. We boarded a train and headed north to Townsville, also in Queensland and about 800 miles from Brisbane. The trains in Australia have improved immensely since those World War II years, but in 1943 that rail thing was so rinky-dink that we dubbed it the "Toonerville Trolley." It was more like an outdated street car. After several days, we finally made it to Townsville.

This time we set up our tents in a city park only a few blocks from the Message Center which was located on the second floor of a building on main street downtown. Townsville was a very nice town with three theatres, a number of restaurants including several "fast food" fish and chip joints, and an ample number of pubs.

Considering there was a war raging to the north, we were most content to drop anchor at least for a while in that small coastal town that was appropriately named. In a current World-Atlas, Townsville is listed at a population of 58,847, not counting the aborigines that may wander down from the north from time to time. I am certain that the population of Townsville during WWII was considerably less. I would compare it with a town like Waynesboro, Virginia, with a population at the time of somewhere around 25 to 30 thousand.

One of those Townsville natives was a young lady named Doreen Ellis, whose father was a fisherman and also owned the Ice House and three fish 'n chips style restaurants. They weren't sit-down restaurants, but more like a take-out place. The one that I patronized was a long and narrow room, like a diner without the stools. Doreen would cook the fish and the potatoes, place them on newspapers on the counter and then collect your shillings for whatever the amount. (The monetary system in Australia in those days was the British pound and shilling and I never got the hang of it. I understand they now use the dollar.)

After the serving, the customer could wrap the newspaper around his food to take on his way or he could eat it standing at the counter. Well, this was certainly a new experience for me – not exactly a formal dinner at the Waldorf – but hey, this was life in Townsville and much of Australia for that matter. Who am I to judge, I kind of liked the idea.

Another custom that really took getting used to was driving on the left side of the road, and having the steering wheel on the right side. Well it's all in what you get accustomed to, and at that young age all of life was new to me and I loved it.

The major motion picture theatre in Townsville reminded me of the Paramount Theatre in Charlottesville. It was a larger theatre but very wide like the Paramount. All of the seats were reserved and for very good reason. The house was sold out almost every night. The theatre also had an organ and the Aussies loved to sing along. A "first-run" theatre with a double feature and two news reels, Movietone News before the first feature and Paramount News before the second. As a long time movie buff, this arrangement was much to my liking!

Movies have always done well in Australia and particularly in Townsville. With the influx of American servicemen the attendance grew considerably. Since most of the movies were shown at night it was imperative that you made a reservation. There was a small church in the residential section of town only a block from our camping area. Since the building was only being used one day a week, the enterprising young preacher moved the pulpit back, put up a movie screen, enclosed the area in the back of the balcony and put in two new 35mm movie projectors. They didn't change anything else. His wife would sit by the church door and sell tickets, and voila! Townsville's first neighborhood theatre! We sat in the church pews and occasionally prayed that the flicks would get better, but with some of the movies even that didn't help! Anyway, we laughed a lot. At that young age and with those crazy galoots we made fun of everything.

There was an area completely surrounded by water just off the coast of Townsville called Magnetic Island. It had a sandy beach for the swimmers (my friend Doreen was one of the best),

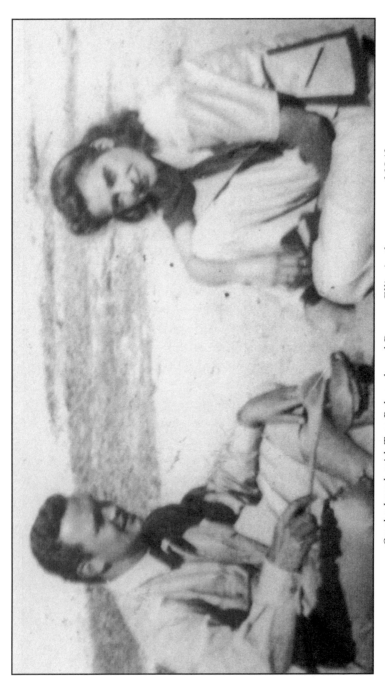

On the beach with Tom Behrendt and Doreen Ellis, in the summer of 1943.
Photo taken on Magnetic Island off the coast of Townsville, Queensland, Australia.

*Doreen Ellis on the rocks of Magnetic Island in Queensland
of Australia. Magnetic Island is off the coast of Townsville.
Photo taken by Tom Behrendt in 1943.*

Tom Behrendt and Doreen Ellis on the beach of Magnetic Island,
just off the coast of Townsville, Queensland in Austrailia in 1943.

a picnic area, hiking area, a few private homes and an old two-story hotel. If you have ever seen the hotel at Orkney Springs, Virginia, you would know exactly what this hotel looked like. It was built prior to the turn of the century and in those days, it was the best the area had to offer. Doreen packed a picnic lunch and the two of us, bathing suits in hand, got on the ferry and sailed out to spend the day away from the army. We went swimming, ate our picnic lunch, hiked over the rocks on the other part of the island, took pictures and then had dinner in the dining room of the hotel before returning to the mainland on the boat's final run for the day.

That was the type of day that would help me endure the future. Pleasant memories are the best when they are recent, and those lovely memories of Magnetic Island would be the most recent to me for the next two years. The messages that we were receiving in the Townsville Message Center indicated that we were about to move out into a combat area.

U.S. Army Photo

Coming Ashore, Lingayen Gulf – Luzon.

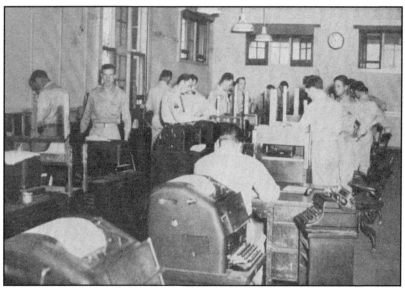

U.S. Army Photo

Teletype Room, Signal Center, Sommerville House,
Brisband, Queensland, Australia

U.S. Army Photo

Signal Corps Training

Chapter 5

OFF TO THE WAR
AND POINTS NORTH

It was now time for us to leave Australia and head north to New Guinea. After we had boarded our equipment on the ship, we headed south for a short time in order to get around the Great Barrier Reef. We sailed out through the Capricorn Channel and then north into the Coral Sea toward Port Moresby.

We were in the Coral Sea for over 800 miles. For most of that time, the sea was as rough as we had ever seen. For all of one day and some of another day, everybody on that boat was throwing up. Never have I seen so many sick people, including myself. We couldn't eat anything because it wouldn't stay down. Most of that would end up on the deck of the ship so nobody could walk any distance at all without the fear of slipping and falling on the vomit. At my age now I have a fear of falling but at least it would probably be a clean fall. But on that deck with all those sick G.I.'s, everyone was deathly afraid of hitting the deck!

The funny thing about all of this is that it was a perfectly beautiful day. The sun was shining, the sky was blue with only a few puffy white clouds passing by. But down near the water, the wind was blowing and the sea seemed to be in a state of turmoil, slopping around in every direction. The waves looked confused and excited as if they didn't know which way to go. As a result our ship was not only going up and down but swinging side to side as well. I meant to ask one of the crew members if this was the same on every trip but I couldn't find one that wasn't hanging over the side. You couldn't find anybody that had a lot to say. I don't know if the ship's pilot was sick but he had the wheel and the compass to hold on to at least. I didn't wonder until later who the unlucky people were who had to clean that ship. And you think your job is tough!

We finally arrived at Port Moresby near the southern tip of Papua, New Guinea. Whatever the near future held for us, it had to be better than our experiences of the last few days.

When our ship arrived at Port Moresby it was raining. That was good for the crew on that boat because if nothing else it would help wash away some of the vile that covered most of the deck. One may wonder why I am reporting this event to an extent greater than necessary, but this sort of thing only happens to a few people once in their lives, and we thank God for that.

That boat ride did prepare me for the future: going out for a whale watching excursion in a small boat off the coast of Cape Cod was a walk in the park. Boat rides out to Martha's Vineyard and Nantucket seemed as adventurous as swimming across the Cow Pasture River in Millboro Springs, Virginia. (Not very.)

It continued to rain the entire time we were in Port Moresby, and after a few days they shipped us out and it was still raining. Some rain is good but this was ridiculous.

This time we were headed for Goodenough Island (ha ha, it's no joke). It was a very small island south of Port Moresby and east of New Guinea in a much calmer part of the Coral Sea. Goodenough is so small that it's not on most maps, but I can assure you that it's there! Rumor had it that when Amelia Earhart flew over it she blinked and missed it. That threw off her instrument panel and she made a wrong turn, ran out of gas and was lost in the Coral Sea. Now you know why they never found her.

General Headquarters Message Center,
Port Moresby, 6 May 1944

U.S. Army Photo

Leyte Landing

U.S. Army Photo

Mud, Mud, Mud – and lots of it!

Goodenough Island had a number of good features. It was off the beaten path and didn't have the large number of people and all the confusion that was so prevalent in Port Moresby. It rained part of almost every day but not the entire day. There was a river that came down the mountain right along side our camp-site with fresh cold water. It was really the coldest water I had ever felt. It seemed strange to be in the tropics with this almost freezing water. What an invigorating experience when we waded in to wash our clothes. I wasn't worried about the clothes shrink-ing but I was concerned about the shrinking of parts of my body. You may understand why some of the memories of Goodenough Island are so invigorating, and this was just the beginning.

The climate on Goodenough Island was very pleasant most of the time. The sky was blue, the temperature moderate and usually warm refreshing breezes coming off the ocean. I don't remember seeing any natives. Before we got there it must have been a sanctuary for rare tropical plants and animals. There was a well-traveled path from the message center through the jungle to our mess tent. I would estimate that this trail was approximate-ly 100 yards long. The men would clear an area and put up their own individual tent every dozen feet or so on either side of the trail. Of course, a small area had to be cleared between the tent and the well traveled trail in order to gain access to that main thor-oughfare that led from the work place to the food place. (Simpler said, we were still in the jungle.) After Pete Bowman and I cleared our tent area, we hit the sack.

The next morning we discovered that the area between our tent and the outside trail was completely blocked by a huge spi-der and his web. That big black spider was larger than a soccer ball and his web would completely cover a 5x7 rug. It looked like a scene from a freak movie. Needless to say, Pete and I cleared another path around this monster spider so we could get out of our tent and up to the mess tent. After breakfast we went down to an adjoining outfit of soldiers and borrowed a flame thrower to kill the spider. I don't believe in cruelty to animals, but the spider was in my territory now and there wasn't much else we could do to get him out.

Later that afternoon while reading a book on my cot I heard "ker-plunk" and the whole tent shook. There were many trees overhanging the tent but I knew that sound was not a branch. The sides of the tent were tied up on all sides for better ventilation and as I grabbed my rifle and started to load it, a huge snake came sliding down the rope from the side of the tent down to the stake in the ground. It slithered out into the jungle for about 20 feet, then turned around with head up as if to say "I'm waiting, come on if you want to play." Later that night when I told Pete what had happened he wondered if it was time to change neighborhoods.

An island in the south Pacific named Goodenough. I wonder who named it. What was it good enough for? The Army wanted to spread us out under all the different foliage on some of the smaller islands in order to confuse the Japanese in the event of more air strikes. That doesn't explain the origin of the name, but at the time it was certainly good enough for me!

We all felt a little better being a safe distance from Port Moresby where all the Allied troops and war materials were arriving daily. Our work in the message center was much the same as it had been in Australia and in the States, except for our "free" time which would include writing letters, washing clothes and killing snakes. My tent mate, Pete Bowman, was the repair man for the code machines that we used. He worked mostly the day shift but was of course on call at all hours.

One evening when we both had the night off, we were each stretched out on our cots doing a little reading. There was a single light bulb from the top center of the tent that furnished just enough light. The electric current came from a transformer set up near the mess tent. It was a quiet and peaceful evening in the tropics when I happened to notice a big black snake slithering into the tent. It came across the dirt floor towards the center pole that held up the tent as well as the light. My God he was a big one! It could have wrapped itself around that pole and taken it with him. I don't know what type of snake it was and didn't have anybody to ask. Pete must have seen him about the same time as I did and without wasting a second said "it's your turn!" and then continued to read his book. (Wonder if he would have said that had it been a Japanese soldier who had come in our tent?) It was certainly no time to quibble, so I grabbed my machete and chopped that poor snake into a dozen pieces. Thinking about it now, it seems cruel but I don't think I had much of a choice.

The next day, we told this story about our uninvited guest to our co-workers in the message center and found that they all had similar stories to relate to us about their snakes and spiders. It dawned on me that we were doing the same thing to these creatures that the Japanese had been doing to humans for many years: forcing them out of their native land.

Wewak and Madang were villages farther up the northeastern coast of New Guinea. They had just recently been occupied by American forces and were still encountering some Japanese resistance. It appears that one of the final Japanese Kamikaze groups stormed the message center in Madang, killing at least 15 of its occupants including four cryptographers. The Kamikaze soldiers must have been crazy. They were hell bent on destroying everything in sight and killing as many Americans as possible before getting their own heads blown off. Of course they all died, but they succeeded in leaving our camp in a royal mess.

In a matter of days, backup groups from Port Moresby were sent to the area to restore some organization. They sent for four of our cryptographers on Goodenough. In fact, they flew a plane over to pick us up post haste! They sent an old C-47 troop carrier that landed in an open field. There was no air strip at that time on the island. At the time I thought that this was a little above the call of duty, but what the hell. It's the only way to look at it when you have no choice in the matter. At least we were leaving the snakes. The old plane took off through that bumpy field and we breathed a sigh of relief when it finally became airborne.

It was probably 500 miles from Goodenough to Madang so it didn't take too long. They did have an air strip at Madang, thank God. After a nice smooth landing we left the plane and waited to the side of the strip for someone to pick us up. A Signal Corps jeep arrived a while later to greet us and deliver us to the area of the message center and the living quarters. They put us in

the same tent that had been occupied by the code men that had
been shot just a few days earlier. (That was not a comforting
feeling, I must say).

After helping them restore the facilities at Madang, it wasn't
too long before plans were being made for our next invasion:
Hollandia in Dutch New Guinea.

For the record, the New Guinea or Dutch name was actually
Djajapura - but in English it was Hollandia. Also, Hollandia is in
the top half of New Guinea and is owned by the Dutch, hence the
name Djajapura.

There in Papua New Guinea (the bottom half) the dust was
beginning to settle with the war over for those people.

When I look at a map of the area, I'm amazed at the number
of small islands there are in that part of the wold, between
Australia and the Philippines. The Solomon Islands to the east of
New Guinea and Borneo and the island of Indonesia to the west.
There are hundreds of small islands in every shape and size.
People live on these islands without a lot of modern conveniences. Imagine day to day living with no newspapers, television
or even radio. (About the only thing they have is sun and sex and
too much of either one could kill you. Of course, too much of
everything we have in the states can be lethal, so who's better
off?) Those natives would probably get along just fine as they
always had if the Americans or the Japanese don't drop a bomb
on them. It's truly a shame the misery that innocent people have
to endure during wartime.

After sailing up the Solomon Sea, all of our men were ready
for the landing at Hollandia.

The boat ride from our previous location in New Guinea up
to Hollandia was about 500 miles or so in the relatively calm sea.

There were many American boats that sailed into the bay to
invade Djajapura (Hollandia), but not a shot was fired. No sounds
were heard at all. What had happened? It turned out the Japanese
had already gone! Evidently they thought we were going to sail
in to an area several hundred miles to the south, so they moved all
of their troops and equipment there several days before we
arrived. That was the best news we had heard in a long time.

To this day I don't know if it was part of MacArthur's brilliant strategy or simply the ignorance of the Japanese. Either way it worked out well for us.

Hollandia had the most beautiful beach I had ever seen in all of New Guinea. The tent area and the places for the message center and the mess hall had all been cleared months before we got there. It appears the Japanese had used this area as a more permanent base in the early months of the war. In any case, it was ours now and we made the best of it. Unfortunately, the war must go on and in a few weeks, we were loading up for the Philippines. There had been much talk about Roosevelt wanting to by-pass the Philippines but General MacArthur wouldn't permit it. He had told the Filipino's that he would return so we had to load up and make sure that he made it. With our help he did just that. We were on our way to Leyte.

U.S. Army Photo

Typical Signal Field Operations.

Signal Corps Troops laying in wire.
Leyte, 1944

Results of a Japanese Banzi charge.

War is hell. There are times however,
when we have all the conveniences of home!

Jim McNeely, Tom Behrendt and Pete Bowman reading
"Guinea Gold" in San Fernando in 1945.

Chapter 6

BACK TO THE PHILIPPINES
WITH MacARTHUR

In the Philippines.
The first day...landing on the Island of Leyte.

In the early morning hours of October 1944, our troop ship slowly glided into the bay on the Island of Leyte in the Philippines. As I remember, the morning was slightly overcast and still except for the sounds of heavy gunfire over palm and coconut trees in this otherwise beautiful setting. Had there been any native huts in the area, they were long gone by now.

This was "D-1" (Invasion Day plus one) of the American Invasion of the Philippine Islands in the South Pacific. After heavy bombing by the Air Force and shelling from the American Fleet, the Infantry landed. This was D-Day, the day the American Infantry Soldiers went into direct combat with the Japanese Infantry. The fighting was fierce – probably far more intense than General MacArthur had anticipated. I was a member of the Signal Corps., and we had the job of setting up a communications post after our Infantry had cleared out the enemy.

When we landed, our men were still firing at the relentless Japanese forces, who had been on the island for more than two years and were much more familiar with its terrain. At that moment I felt a very strong kinship with those great guys of the Infantry. Many strong emotions came over me while trying to make myself as invisible as possible stretched out prone in the dirt and sand, while the American Infantry was trading fire with our fellow man. (Of course, it was difficult to think of the Japanese as our fellow man at the time, we considered them maniacs who were trying to take over the world.) As darkness approached, the firing subsided and with it began a steady rain that would continue for hours. I dug a foxhole so there would be no outline of my body against the dark background whenever there was lightening or a flash from any remaining gunfire. As my bed for the night filled with water, I remember putting my leather wallet under my helmet so the water wouldn't ruin it. We were all barely holding on to that edge of the island that night, surrounded by an enemy that was hell-bent on killing us all in the name of their Emperor. I must say, without hesitation, that there wasn't a wave of movement coming from my foxhole that long night.

D+2

It was now D+2 that we Americans had returned to the Philippines. I had survived the long, wet night in my foxhole by trying to visualize being in my bathtub at home with the tub overloaded with water, and I eventually fell asleep. It is amazing when I think of all the challenges one can overcome when young in years.

This new day on Leyte was beautiful. The gunfire had subsided for the moment, then out of the blue appeared a huge Japanese plane flying at a very low altitude and very close to our temporary campsite. It appeared to be either attempting to land or trying to gain altitude because it was going so slow. Just then one of our artillery shells hit it in its underbelly and the plane exploded into a million pieces. We hurriedly took whatever cover we could find as huge sections of the plane and parts of Japanese bodies came raining down upon us. It was unimaginable, seeing an arm or a leg or a completely severed head bouncing on the ground in front of me. An image I'll never forget.

A short time later, a young Filipino boy around 13 or 14 years old came directly to me and asked if I would go with him into the next section of the jungle. This young boy took me by the hand and pleaded that I go with him. The others in our group stayed put but I was curious, and thought it wouldn't hurt to check it out. After going with him a short distance through the underbrush, we came to an opening about half the size of a tennis court with weeds about ankle deep. In the center of this opening was a waist-high "stack" of dead Japanese soldiers. There must have been at least 70 or 80 men stacked very neatly one on top of the other in the form of a pyramid, covering about 25 feet. I have no proof of how they were killed, but can only assume the Filipino natives did some fighting on their own. The boy did not speak English, but he was trying hard to communicate with me. I finally understood that he was asking me to get some gasoline in order to cremate the bodies. We then walked back to my group of men and got a spare can of gasoline off one of the jeeps. We took it back through the underbrush to the opening and proceeded to pour it over the bodies. Someone struck a match, and right in front of us it looked and felt like hell on earth. Even though those bodies had been soaked with moisture from the rain the night before, the gasoline soaked through it all and when lit became one huge inferno. It singed some of the nearby vegetation and produced a huge billow of smoke that could have been read by native Indians on the adjacent islands.

Shortly after the initial explosion, I noticed a hand grenade hooked on the belt of one of the bodies. I pointed and yelled "GRENADE!" and my young friend and I took off through the jungle and back to our temporary campsite. Several more explosions came from the pile just as we reached a safe distance. As we walked back into the camp area, one of the men wanted to know if there were any Japanese soldiers over there. After my nod, he exclaimed "Man, you were lucky to get away!

Getting ready to "Hit the Beach."

Our new home away from home.

How many are there?" I told him about 80 or so but not to worry as they were all dead. I was surprised to notice then that my new-found little friend did understand some English. After my last remark I looked down at him and saw on his face a most pleased and satisfied grin.

So far there hadn't been a dull moment on the beautiful south sea island of Leyte. The Japanese wanted to keep us active and to earn their respect as they still would not surrender.

Later that 2nd day as we finished our mid-day meal of bare-ly edible K-rations, a Japanese plane flew directly over our group at a very low altitude and opened fire with a machine gun. We were in an open field and the bullets were flying in all direc-tions. I remember diving into some tall wild-grass in hopes that the enemy couldn't see me as the machine gun bullets pelted the sandy soil around me. The plane was so low I could have hit it with a rock. As it passed over the horizon, we heard a loud explo-sion followed by our collective sigh of relief as that lone ranger rode into the sunset. For him, I assume it was his final push – firing all of his bullets at us before diving his plane to the ground. A futile effort against an enemy he could not defeat.

In the following days, we moved our campsite inland to set up a semi-permanent message center. We put up our tents, dug wells so we could take showers and built latrines. Like it or not, this was to be our home for an indefinite period. After the dust settled and we began taking shifts in the code room of the mes-sage center, things almost became a routine except for an occa-sional Japanese air raid. They usually occurred during the early evening hours, before midnight, when there was more activity in the camp. You could depend on a visit during a full moon. Without today's modern technology, they would fly over late at night and simply count the number of tents in an effort to deter-mine the American buildup on that part of the island.

There was one small plane that would fly over every moon-lit night. He was doing more spying that firing and we didn't fire at him. The plane was probably going less than 45 miles per hour and sounded like a 1938 Ford pickup in desperate need of a ring job. The pilot put in such a regular appearance that we named him the Lone Ranger and some even called him Lonesome George. On those moonlit nights when the plane was clearly visible, some of us would go out into the open area around the tents and actually wave to the pilot. I don't know if he saw us or not, but it was our way of saying "Better go home George before your flying crate falls apart!" Ah, the lighter moments of war.

The Filipino people were very grateful to us for driving the Japanese out of their island and strove to show their appreciation in numerous ways. The women washed our clothes and gave us home-cooked meals. The men helped in construction of the message center, repaired the dirt roads, and dug wells and latrines.

During any conflict when you return to an area to flush out the enemy, it is most desirable to have the natives on your side - and they certainly were in the Philippines. (It was the Filipinos, after all, who must have been responsible for the huge pyramid of dead Japanese soldiers we discovered on our second day on Leyte.)

As the weeks went by, we Americans became more accustomed to living on Leyte with our friends the Filipinos. These natives had little to offer in the form of entertainment since they were far more interested in us than we were in them. When our group of code men weren't working in the message center we would probably be playing poker, shooting crap or writing letters home. There was a guy in our group that had a small record player and many times, especially at night, we listened to the great music of Tommy Dorsey, Glenn Miller, Harry James and other great bands of the era. These were all forms of entertainment and activity that the G.I.'s created for each other to pass the time. For me, the greatest entertainment of all was the movies that the Special Services branch of the War Department provided. They furnished many of the Company's who were serving in combat areas with 35mm movie projectors and Hollywood furnished the movies. I can't say for sure how many movies I saw while sitting on a log in the middle of a jungle. They were a great pastime for us, and became a real oddity for the natives of Leyte, who had never seen a movie.

I remember my father taking me to my first movie when I was seven years old. The new Lafayette Theatre in Charlottesville,

Virginia was crowded and we sat in the fourth or fifth row. My head was touching the back of the seat as I looked up at that big screen and wondered how all those running horses stayed up there. I was sure that the thundering herd was coming down on top of us. This experience came to mind as I watched the Filipinos dodge the bullets coming from our movie screen.

On many of these nights, we had to shut down the projector as the Japanese reminded us that we were at war. The sirens would ring out at least once during almost every movie. All lights would go out and we would run to the nearest foxhole (which proved to be a damn nuisance, especially if it was a good movie). Fortunately for us they would drop their bombs near an airstrip or where they thought the munitions were stored. If they didn't stay too long and the "all clear" was sounded, we would return to our logs and finish watching the likes of Fred Astaire and Ginger Rogers on the big screen.

Most young men in their teens or early twenty's have not had the time to get accustomed to luxury living. (The ones who did fall into that category probably had enough family influence and money to keep then out of combat.) These were the fine young men from average American families who really wanted to do whatever they could to eliminate the enemy who had bombed Pearl Harbor and forced Americans out of the Philippines. We could not tolerate the unbelievable actions of a foreign country that most of us knew little about.

When the Japanese bombed Pearl Harbor on December 7th, 1941, I would never have believed that I would go to the Philippines and later Japan in 1945.

At this point in our travel abroad the situation had become less hectic and more routine. We were getting accustomed to our country style living on the sweet little island of Leyte and rather dreaded what the future held. Several young Filipinos from a nearby village dug a new well for us, as well as another latrine and several more fox holes. They were always willing to do whatever they could to show their appreciation for our returning to their country and forcing out the Japanese.

I experienced a heart-warming incident many years after the

Barney Gullickson standing in front of what's left of the Ideal Theatre in downtown Manila in 1945.

war on an Epcot Center shuttle bus in Florida. I happened to be seated next to a Filipino gentleman much younger than I, and we struck up a conversation. He was so pleased to learn that I was among the group of Americans that had returned to the Philippines and fought on their behalf. It was fifty years after the war and this young gentleman shook my hand and said, "Thank you so much for giving our country back to us!" That statement, from a native of the Philippines, was without a doubt one of the most cherished forms of gratitude I have ever received. As most G.I.'s don't get a lot of gratitude, that comment really restored my faith in mankind. Ever since that chance meeting on the shuttle bus, I am constantly reminded that there are many good people on this earth, you just have to open your eyes.

As a rule, young people do not think too far in the future. Live today for what it's worth and tomorrow will take care of itself. Umm...not a bad way to go, at least for young people who haven't yet taken on the responsibilities of the world. Choosing a career, getting married, raising children, buying a house. In the Philippines we didn't have any of those challenges. All we had to worry about was staying alive and healthy. The army provided doctors if we needed them, food and cooks to prepare it (but you must take the army's word for it) tents to sleep in and trucks to ride in. Life on the Island of Leyte really wasn't all that bad. We familiarized ourselves with their culture and they with ours, and we all made the necessary adjustments. Quite well, I might add. Then, the time came when we had to move on to the next adventure. As Fitzpatrick used to say in his 1930's Travelogues, "The time has come when we must bid farewell to the village of Tacloban and the gentle people here on the beautiful island of Leyte in the southern Philippines." It was a great experience for us but unfortunately, the war continued and it was time for our next move.

We now prepared for the invasion of Luzon and the capital city of Manila! We headed southwest through the Mindanao Sea and then southeast of Palawan into the Sulu Sea. It was there that we joined a huge convoy that was making preparations to sail up the western side of the Philippines and into the South China Sea

Roy James and Barney Gullickson walking in the less damaged part of downtown Manila.

west of the main island of Luzon. The convoy was headed for Luzon and would land about halfway up the island in a place known as Lingayen Gulf, a hundred miles north of Manila. From our starting point on Leyte to the Lingayen Gulf, the trip covered approximately 800 miles. We were all looking forward to a pleasant two or three days voyage, but the Japanese had other ideas.

On a relatively quiet and uneventful day at sea, suddenly there appeared three small Japanese planes very high in the sky. They were like bees buzzing around trying to decide whether or not to go in the hive. They buzzed around for several minutes, apparently deciding which ships to zero in on. They were too high for our anti-aircraft guns to reach them, so we were forced to sit and wait. Our entire convoy was continuing to sail along at its designated speed. For a moment or two we pretended to ignore them, but we were ready. The Japanese had quite a selection of targets from which to choose as our convoy consisted of approximately sixty to eighty ships transporting men from different branches of the service. We were also transporting equipment from these different branches, battleships and other Navy big guns to insure a successful landing.

Finally, one of the planes left the group and headed straight down to one of the Navy ships on the eastern side of the convoy. The anti-aircraft guns from all of the ships began pouring thousands of bullets into that plane. The pilot must have been dead long before the plane ever hit one of our ships. There were several loud explosions and the ship was damaged to such an extent that it had to drop out of the convoy.

Right after that, another Japanese plane flew to the center of the convoy. He had obviously set the automatic pilot to strike the designated ship and them simply waited to die. Our American gunners were doing a fine job as best they could with unbelievable rapid speed. In their tremendous effort to knock out the planes, they continued to fire even when the plane hit the ship, sending hundreds of stray bullets over the designated target and into the side of many of our own ships. I fell to the deck and crawled over the ship's steel siding when I heard the tracer

Barney, David and Roy and their covered king size fox hole on Leyte in 1944.

*Tom Behrendt viewing some of the ruins
in downtown Manila in 1945.*

bullets banging into the side of our ship. I certainly didn't want to lose my life from friendly fire and was grateful that it lasted only a few minutes.

I must note that I wondered later why the Japanese didn't attack with all three planes at once. Our anti-aircraft gunners would have been much less effective if they had three planes to shoot at all at once rather than one at a time. I can only assume doing it separately was their moment of glory before they ended their lives. And speaking of that, it is difficult for me to imagine that a healthy and vibrant young man, piloting a single engine plane on a beautiful sunny afternoon over the South China Sea, would dive his plane into one of our ships in an effort to slow down one ship and kill maybe a few men. The Japanese did just that many times and three times to us in a single afternoon.

Now the third and final plane picked out his target ship and headed for what would be his final hurrah. Our gunners were especially prepared for this one and every gunner on every ship began firing as soon as the plane appeared in their sights. The barrage of gunfire was so fierce that the plane exploded in mid air. It was quite a sight and I've never heard so many cheers in my life. The plane disintegrated like 4th of July fireworks and scattered in a million pieces over the South China Sea. It was a beautiful ending to a futile attempt by the Japanese to stop some very determined Americans on their return to the Philippines. Of course, we'd already been on Leyte, but when you head to Luzon and proceed to overtake Manila, the pearl of the South Pacific, you are in the big leagues of war. Those of us in this convoy who were to be the D+1 landing force on Luzon, were very happy to know that there would be three less Japanese planes to attack us when we landed at Lingayen Gulf.

Luzon is an elongated island somewhat in the shape of a contorted foot. Assuming the top of the foot is facing north, Manila is at the heel, on the western side with Manila Bay in the South China Sea. Lingayen Gulf is north of Manila Bay, about half the length of the island. The eastern side of the island is the Philippine Sea in the Pacific Ocean.

Our ship pulled into Lingayen Gulf late in the afternoon and waited in the Bay until dark. We could hear firing to the south during the daylight hours but after dark it subsided considerably. We then climbed down the side of our ship into smaller boats that took us to the beach. It was a dark night and we couldn't see much, but what we could see was a huge American "big gun" that the Japanese were firing at us! We were later told that the gun was originally put in a cave during World War I by the Americans in an effort to protect the Filipinos from any foreign invasion. Whether or not it was used during that time is a mystery, but when the Japanese invaded the Philippines, Manila and all of Luzon, they also took over the mountain and the cave housing this American big gun. General MacArthur was determined to get it all back and with a lot of luck and determination, we finally did.

Our Infantry had landed the day before and managed to drive on into the flat lands in the southern half of the island almost out of reach of the range of that big gun. The gun was on wheels so it could be rolled out and used at night and then put back in the cave to hide it during the day. It was rolled out that night and the Japanese fired it in that southerly direction not realizing that more Allied troops had landed during the night and were in foxholes on the beach directly below them. In our haste to find cover we found a foxhole big enough for one man and three of us dived into it. I don't know if we were friends at the time but we certainly were before the night was over. Those Japanese fired that gun all night as we could hear the shells whistling overhead. Fortunately for us they must have been firing at our Infantry Regiment and the invasion equipment that had gone on ahead of us. We didn't fire back because we couldn't see where the shells were coming from. The next day, however, was a different story.

That next morning a spotter aircraft from one of our Navy ships flew over the area and spotted the tracks that appeared to be coming out of the side of the mountain. The entrance to the cave was covered with foliage and the big gun was completely hidden, but not for long. I don't know how much damage that cannon did but it was something that had to be eliminated.

The next day we watched and listened on our radio to the pilot of our spotter plane giving instructions to the gunner on our battleship the exact location of the cave. The guns on the battleship fired and after a few near misses - bang! - right on target! The door and all the foliage went flying in all directions. Then we heard the spotter pilot say "That's a bullseye! Now put another one in there to make sure the gun is crippled!" This next shot went past the destroyed doors and exploded in the cave. There couldn't have been anything left of that gun when that shell exploded. The whole mountain shook. And then after several minutes, after all the rubble had fallen and the dust had settled, there was a tremendous HURRAH from all the happy American G.I.'s. (The happy cheers sounded like the sounds coming from Scott Stadium at the University of Virginia if the Cavaliers scored a touchdown.)

Getting rid of that gun just about eliminated all of the Japanese resistance at Lingayen Gulf. More troops arrived that afternoon to secure the Allied takeover of the area, and more equipment arrived including the big trucks that took us on to our new destination.

The next morning proved to be the start of an absolutely beautiful day. After our K-Rations breakfast, we loaded the trucks and headed south. In the distance to the west was a beautiful mountain range that reminded me of the many times I had seen the Blue Ridge Mountains in Virginia while driving from Washington D.C. to Charlottesville. The weather was perfect. On such a beautiful day it was hard to believe we were in the midst of a war. The Japanese at Lingayen were all gone, and the ones in Manila were putting up a fierce battle to hold on to that city and the tip end of Luzon. The American forces had landed at Manila Bay a few days earlier and now our forces had arrived to help force out the enemy.

My group of code machine operators along with the other groups of Signal Corps men were assigned to set up operations in the town of San Fernando about 20 or so miles north of Manila. This was a pleasant village that showed no signs of ever having been occupied by the Japanese. We set up our Message

Center in a small wooden structure that at one time appeared to be a library. We put up our tents nearby in a large park near the center of town. It was a nice situation because it was centralized in the heart of town and we were able to use some of the buildings currently in use by the people of San Fernando. Of course, the Army paid these people for the use of their property, which in turn made them love us all the more.

When the American forces arrived in a small, sleepy country village on an island in the south Pacific, it is somewhat like a circus: marching bands, big loaded trucks and all the people and paraphernalia that go with it. We put on a show the likes of which they have never seen. This was a big event in their lives, to say the least, and to get paid for the use of some of their property was unbelievable. That was one of the reasons they were so nice to us, along with what appeared to be a genuine affection toward Americans.

For the most part, American soldiers then were a happy bunch with magnetic personalities and a sense of humor that endeared them to all of those who wanted to be a friend.

When I was a cadet at Augusta Military Academy in Virginia in the late 30's, I had a friend who was from Manila. His name was Kenneth Coote. He and his brother Leonard had been sent there by their parents in an effort to get them a better education than they would have gotten during those days in Manila. Their father was in the diplomatic branch of the U.S. government and had been stationed in the Philippines for many years. When Leonard graduated in June of 1941, both boys returned to Manila to be with their parents. Six months later the Japanese made their infamous attack on Pearl Harbor and it was the beginning of our participation in World War II. The Japanese then invaded the Philippines and when they took over Manila they ordered all Americans to be imprisoned in a place called Santo Tomas. (That is, all American civilians that could possibly disrupt the Japanese effort in the days ahead.) Since the Coote's father was in the American Diplomatic Corps and the two boys had just returned from a military school in America, it seemed obvious under the

Staff of the message center still together after landing on Leyte in 1944.

U.S. Army Photo

Jungle Combat – Leyte, 1944

U.S. Army Photo

Signal Unit Operations – Leyte, 1944

Shot to Pieces

By the time American troops had overpowered the Japanese defending Manila, this once beautiful city was shot to pieces. American GIs who spearheaded the attack through the center of Manila, and who were relieved after 16 days of fighting from building to building, pass through the Pace (Peace) section.

circumstances that this entire family would have been imprisoned in Santo Tomas. It was my second day in San Fernando and I was already very determined to eventually get to Manila to check it out.

As the American infantry were trudging through Manila, the Japanese were setting fire to everything in sight and particularly the government buildings, many of which had been built by the Americans in the past twenty years. As the last group of Japanese soldiers rushed to get on the last boat leaving Manila bay, the city of Manila was in flames. From all accounts it resembled Atlanta near the end of the Civil War or the great earthquake in San Francisco. There were reports of extreme cruelty by the Japanese, like killing women and children in their homes as they fled the island. They seemed to have no regard for the well being of others, including themselves. In combat they reminded me of robots existing only to serve their master, whether their actions made any sense or not. Thank God our country's forces finally rid Manila and all of the Philippine Islands of the Japanese forces. The Filipinos were eternally grateful, and those of us in the American army could now begin to make preparations for the invasion of Japan.

We had set up in San Fernando for what we all hoped would be a lengthy stay. It can be quite the operation to create a message center, with various pieces of equipment arriving daily at the new location and all the manpower needed to make it work. Unlike when a circus comes to town in the U.S., they set up in one day and leave the next. It takes us a little longer and we like to stay a little longer. I think we were in San Fernando for a period of over six months. When we did leave, we left millions of dollars worth of equipment for the Filipinos to play with. If you happen to see a video of Manila today, notice all the colorful, dressed up and decorated jeeps roaming the streets. They are the off spring of the ones we left.

We finally got operations running smoothly in San Fernando and in April 1945 we learned that President Roosevelt had died at his retreat in Warm Springs, Georgia. This was quite a shock to the American Servicemen. President Roosevelt had been in office for almost three full terms, and that was half of most of these American soldiers' lifetimes. We had lost the only leader most of us had ever known, and it was quite a blow. Unfortunately, we didn't have high hopes for his predecessor, Harry S. Truman. We would find out later, however, the greatest thing he ever did in order to save the lives of thousands and thousands of American soldiers. In my mind and other's, Mr. Truman turned out to be one of the best leaders.

Now it was time for me to go to Manila and see what I could find out about my friend Kenneth Coote. I arrived early in the afternoon and was promptly informed by one of the locals that all of the people at the infamous Santo Tomas had gone. He didn't believe anybody was still there, but he gave me directions and I went anyway. I guess he was right because the only person I could find was a middle-aged Filipino also looking for an American friend that had been imprisoned there when the war had first started. He hadn't had any luck either, and said he thought they all had died. There were no records to be found. We talked for quite a while, I believe his name was Roland or Rolando. He took me to his home to meet his family. They were all very nice to me. They were the first friends I met in Manila, and there were more to come.

I was back the next day with my group of cryptographers at our newly constructed message center in San Fernando. These were a great group of guys but they didn't like to venture out very much. They preferred to stay close to Mother (Mother being the message center, the mess hall and their bunks). They did, however, want to know all about Manila. I told them that I didn't have time to see much on my first trip but that I was going back the next weekend and I'd give them a full report.

We had new men join our group as time went by and I don't remember all of their names, but the four of us that were together the longest were Dave Graves from Brooklyn, Roy James from New Jersey, Jim MacNeely from South Philadelphia, and myself from Charlottesville, Virginia. We had been together since our basic training in Sea Girt, New Jersey.

There were several other men I remember well. One G.I. suffered mental problems and had to return to the states, two others were sent back because of illness, one died in New Guinea of a disease called Scrub-Tifus, one died of Malaria, and one died on the ship going from Leyte to Luzon when the bullet from an American gunner on another ship ricocheted and hit him.

If not for a fair amount of good luck, most of us wouldn't be here. I think I would rather have luck on my side than either health or wealth. Health and wealth are important, but I have known healthier and wealthier men who are already gone from this earth.

The week finally rolled by and I got my second chance to visit Manila. I had to wait until I got off duty at four, making it after five by the time I got there. The town was swinging with American G.I.'s and Filipino girls everywhere. I milled around the center of town for a time trying to decide what to do, and finally made a decision but unfortunately it turned out to be a bad one. (No one has good luck all the time). I went in to a Filipino bar inhabited by lots of happy, friendly American soldiers who were laughing and joking and having a great time. I sat at the bar and ordered a drink. God only knows what was in that glass because before I could even order a second round I became sick as a dog. It was a terrible feeling with my head going round and round, and my stomach going the other way. Everybody else at the bar seemed to be having such a good time, I could not figure out why I was so ill.

Sick and embarrassed, I slid off the barstool and made my way over to the door. Once out on the sidewalk I searched for a place away from the crowds so I could lie down and "die." I made my way slowly down the sidewalk until I came to a ladies dress shop. It was dimly lit but there was a sign on the glass door that said that they were open. I walked in and passed several glass display cases on my way to the back of the store. There were two women in the shop, an employee and her customer. They didn't say any thing to me but I am sure they must have wondered what was going on. When I got to the last display case, I went and laid down behind it where it was dark and promptly fell asleep. The women must not have wondered too

This family of Filippinos adopted our group of friends and took us into their homes in San Fernando, a few miles north of Manila, on Luzon in 1945.

long before they called the Military Police. I don't know how long I had been there when I felt something poking at my side. The room was brighter and there were two men in uniform standing above me wearing highly polished black shoes and neat uniforms with the letters MP on their sleeves. "Come on fella, let's get up" was the first thing I heard. When I didn't respond immediately, they gently picked me up. I then explained what had happened and that I still felt like hell and really needed to go back to sleep. "Well, you can't do it in here, so you come on with us." They led me out of the store, into their jeep outside and it was off to jail for me. There was a time in my life when I dreamed of being in the "Pearl of the South Pacific," but certainly never under these conditions.

The jail was just a few blocks away but the street was filled with huge potholes which kept the jeep bouncing up and down. Being sick wasn't enough, this was cruel and extreme punishment for a guy whose only crime was a bad drink. Those M.P.'s didn't realize how lucky they were that I didn't have to throw up on their backs. We got to the jail and when the jeep stopped, I finally thought I might live. At that point I was anxious to get inside to get some peace and quiet.

The two sets of highly polished shoes ushered me in and up to the Desk Sergeant and explained to him why I was there. After requesting my name, serial number and whatever else, he had his "heavy" usher me down the narrow hall and into a cell. An empty cell with absolutely nothing in it. It was clean and bright but that was it. I remember wooden floors, high wooden walls, no windows and not even a steel bunk chained to the wall. I didn't expect a Holiday Inn but this was ridiculous. Anyway, I was too tired to worry about it so I laid down in the far corner and fell asleep. It was probably 7 or 8 o'clock in the evening by then.

When I woke I was in for the surprise of my life. The cell was dimly lit and FILLED with people, I think mostly American G.I.'s. It was the biggest mess I had ever experienced. There were guys who had completely passed out and those that hadn't were all very drunk. One was talking to himself, one thought he was singing, two were moaning as though they were in great pain, and they were ALL filthy. Several appeared as though they had been in a fist fight and two others were having a big argument about who stole their money. Another had vomited all over the floor and over the shoe of his friend who had already passed out. I thought some of those people must have been at the bar that I had patronized that evening.

Now that I had most of my faculties back, I looked at my watch and it was almost 2 a.m. I shook the bars of the cell door and called for a guard. A young man appeared with keys in hand and asked me what was the problem. "Look in here. I was put in here earlier because I was sick and needed to lie down, but I can't stay here now. Won't you please let me out?" He said that there was a curfew at 1 a.m. and it was now 2 a.m. "If an M.P. sees you he'll just bring you back and then we'll both be in trouble." I told him that I had friends that live a short distance away and that I was sure that I could get there without being seen. Believe it or not, that fine gentleman let me out the back door and I took off running into the night! I ran through the streets of downtown Manila until I reached the home of my new Filipino friends.

My friend's house was an older, two-story frame structure that he probably inherited from his parents. It was near the downtown area about four or five blocks from the jail and about the same distance south of the bar and dress shop. I knocked on the front door and after a few minutes I heard someone on the other side. "Rolando, it's Tom, The American you met at Santo Tomas last week." He immediately opened the door and invited me in. Considering the time of night, I simply told him that everything was all right and I just needed a place to sleep for a few hours. He took me upstairs into an empty room, unrolled a sleeping mat on the floor, hung a bracket on the wall on which he tied a mosquito net that hung down around the sleeping mat on the floor. All the comforts of home if you lived in a tent in the tropics. They had no window screens, no screen doors and of course, no air conditioning.

I don't think Manila was known as the "Pearl of the Orient" in those days. I remember thinking that a furniture company could make a fortune there because so many places didn't have a stick of furniture. Perhaps the Japanese took it with them.

In any case, I did sleep well, and the next morning proceeded to explain to Mr. and Mrs. Rolando what had happened the night before. Mrs. Rolando suddenly exclaimed "You got sick and went into a shop and fell asleep behind a display counter? I can't believe it was you!" Her husband and I looked at each other wondering what she was talking about. "That was me!" she said. "That was our shop. I was behind the counter when you came in and my friend and I were afraid of what you might do so we summoned the police. I am so sorry – had I known you were sick I would have tried to make your more comfortable." I repeatedly told her not to worry, that 'all's well that ends well'. After thanking them for letting me spend the night, I ventured north back toward San Fernando.

That was a Saturday night I shall never forget. Can you imagine the response I got when I told my friends at the Message Center? They also wouldn't easily forget that story.

Back to the routine of a cryptographer or code machine operator in the Message Center of the U.S. Army Signal Corps. This was the message center for the entire Allied forces operating in the Philippines and throughout the South Pacific in the spring and summer months of 1945. We had finally settled down to working and living in the small village of San Fernando where day to day life really wasn't all that bad.

Some of us continued to venture down to Manila occasionally. My friend Dave and I went one weekend and I showed him the infamous bar and jail, but we didn't go in either. He saw the dress shop and met my friends the Rolando's. There was a movie theatre still in operation in Manila after the Japanese left. With nothing better to do, Dave and I went in to see *"Gung-Ho!"* This was the original *Gung-Ho* with Randolph Scott. It happened to be a war movie with the Americans fighting the Japanese. What a great time to see that movie! The theatre will filled with Americans and Filipinos and there wasn't a moment of silence. When the Americans landed in a Japanese-held island, the Filipino's in the theatre would let out their boisterous approval with loud whoops and hollers over and over again throughout the movie. The dialogue wasn't important and that was just as well because you couldn't hear it anyway. It did my heart good seeing that movie, to know that the Filipinos really were happy to have us back on their land. It was a great feeling, and I could see why General MacArthur did not want to by-pass the Philippines on our way to Japan. He told them we would return, and by God we did.

Many American G.I.'s thought that perhaps MacArthur loved the Filipino's so much that he used us to get him back to a place where he was thought of as a Super Hero. I know that MacArthur was often thought of as a self-centered egotist, and that many Americans did not like him for that reason, but he certainly could get the job done. The Filipino's thought he was a god, and to a great extent he seemed to believe it himself. He really appeared to put himself above the rest of the world, and as we would later find out, the Japanese did too.

Not to get ahead of the story, it is still 1945 and we are still in San Fernando, routinely doing our jobs and wondering just what and where our new orders would take us.

We Americans were making plans to invade Japan. General MacArthur had picked the sights for the landings, the number of men needed for such a huge undertaking, the equipment, tanks, troop landing vehicles and big guns from hundreds of ships of the U.S. Navy. Thousands of planes dropping thousands of bombs for four or five days before the actual landings, and the entire Marine Corps with the parachute unit from every branch of the United States military. Add all this to the Salvation Army, General George Patton, General Eisenhower and all the fighting men from Australia and from China (that's a few million right there) and we might get in.

Imagine for a moment that we had invaded and the Japanese had surrendered and the war ends. Millions of people are dead. General MacArthur comes in and takes over what's left of the country. He is crowned the new Emperor but there aren't enough Japanese to govern. Who can he get to serve him? Also, we Americans would have to do without all those great Japanese creations, cars and big screen televisions and most important, those video cassette recorders! Well, thank God this wasn't the way it turned out.

We of course didn't have to invade Japan. They even invited us in for a visit after we dropped a couple of subtle hints. Those "hints" may have killed thousands and destroyed Hiroshima, but that was a mere drop in the bucket compared to the death of millions of Japanese and Americans and the destruction of the many cities of Japan if we had to invade. That would be unthinkable. Dropping the bomb on Hiroshima and Nagasaki was a terrible thing to have to do, but it was the only way we knew to stop the insanity.

The Special Services department of the U.S. Army published a newspaper in the South Pacific. The first one we saw was called *Guinea Gold*. This was during the time we were in New Guinea. The next one I remember was on Luzon in San Fernando. Pete Bowman, our Service Manager and all-around great guy, came into camp with a fresh new copy on August 6th, 1945. (Remember that date). On the front page on column two or three at the very bottom, in a small space approximately two by two inches, the following was printed: "Air Force drops super bomb on Hiroshima" followed by only a couple of lines about how powerful the bomb was. That was all of the space allotted for the story. Pete and I joked about it while wondering if it could in any way shorten the rest of the war.

That small, leftover space in a newspaper is called a filler, and any little bit of humor or local news is usually used. Apparently, the "super-bomb" story had just come in and instead of changing their front page lead story, they decided to use it as a filler! A huge mistake.

The Atomic Bomb. The Americans had been developing the Atom Bomb for years, with plans to use the first one on Hitler and Nazi Germany. The Russians beat us to Berlin and Hitler's "goose was cooked." When the Joint Chiefs of Staff had appeared in the White House to get approval to use the new Atomic Bomb on Hiroshima, our new President Harry Truman said emphatically: "DROP IT!" I have admired him ever since that day.

The more we heard the better we liked it. Three days later we learned that a second bomb was dropped on Nagasaki. The Japanese had laughed when we told them about the super bomb we were going to use. After Hiroshima they changed nothing. Perhaps they thought it was the only one that we had and they could keep fighting. They must have realized after Nagasaki that we meant business and more bombs were on their way.

White Flag! White Flag! White Flag! The Japanese surrendered very quickly. They didn't want us to do to them what they had done to Manila. What they should have understood is that the bombings of Hiroshima and Nagasaki were small repayments from the United States for what they had done to our fleet at Pearl Harbor. Several days later, the formal Unconditional Surrender was signed on an American battleship in Tokyo Bay with the Japanese warlords and General MacArthur, and the high ranking officials from all branches of the United States Armed Forces that participated in this four year struggle.

U.S. Army Photo

Japanese soldiers surrendering to a U.S. soldier – a rare sight.

*Smiling Jake and Tom (behind wheel) must be
talking about girls in their Jeep on Leyte.*

Tom and Barney on some of the Signal Corps equipment ready to be unpacked. This was our second day on Leyte and there was still much to do.

At a time like this, even those K-Rations tasted pretty good.

Author on Patrol.

My own personal fox hole with handmade cover to keep out the rain.

Tom Behrendt (right) and Barney Gullickson amongst the ruins of Manila.
The Japanese ravished the city as they were forced out in 1945.

Tom Behrendt and Barney Gullickson with three natives a few days after landing on Leyte.

Kenneth Coote from Manila in the Philippine Islands. Cadet at Augusta Military in 1940.

Part of our remaining 1st Signal Team of the 832nd Signal Service Company.
Photo taken on the island of Luzon in San Fernando, 20 miles north of Manila. (1945)

Chapter 7

JAPAN AND HOME . . .

The Japanese had surrendered and the war was over. We were only sorry that President Roosevelt wasn't here to see it, but it still was a great day for all mankind. The way things had been going for the past year or so, I couldn't help but wonder if the Japanese weren't as relieved as we were that the fighting was over.

MacArthur wanted a show of force, a dominant show of force in Japan after the formal surrender was signed. The American G.I.'s were ready to come home, as many had been there for almost three years. But the General wanted us to stay for several reasons, one was to impress the Japanese with our might, and the second and best reason was to give the Americans a chance to actually visit Japan. A wonderful opportunity.

We left Manila bay on a smaller ship, headed north in the South China Sea, then to the east to the Pacific Ocean, then north again to the eastern part of Japan. We went through the Kii Channel and landed at Osaka. It was at night and the entire channel was lit up like Times Square, N.Y. After so many years of darkness it was quite a feeling to see all of those bright cheerful lights.

*Tom Behrendt looking for something to shoot
with a camera in Japan in 1945.*

We disembarked the next day and rode in trucks through the main street of downtown Osaka. We couldn't believe what we saw. The city had been bombed unceasingly for months prior to the surrender and there were thousands of tons of rubble covering the ground as far as the eye could see. And believe it or not, in preparation for our arrival, the Japanese people had actually swept the streets and sidewalks clean as a pin. They were all standing at attention on the sidewalks facing our truck convoy as we slowly rode by. There were hundreds of them, standing four and five deep on each brush-cleaned block for miles through the city.

After all those years of hating the Japanese, I suddenly realized that they could be warm, compassionate and loving human beings, just like us. A nice thought. They were civilians, a different breed than the soldiers and those that started the war. Although they didn't move, I wanted to wave to them and say thanks for cleaning the streets, but the commanding officers told us not to say anything or make any gestures, and it appeared that the Japanese had been told the same thing. In any case, that act of kindness by the Japanese certainly made us feel most welcome, and got us off to a very good start.

After leaving Osaka, the big Army trucks took us on to Kyoto, a city less than fifty miles away. Though the Japanese had just participated in a war, you would never have known it. Much of the rural area between the two cities resembled the rural areas in the U.S. or anywhere else for that matter. The land showed none of the ravages of war since our bombing missions were intended to cripple their ability to make war, not to harm the farms and homes of innocent civilians. We found the same to be true when we arrived in Kyoto, the city of great Oriental religion, with Buddhist temples throughout this original capitol of Japan. This was a truly beautiful place that had escaped the bombing runs of the U.S. Air force. One would never have known there had been a war so close to its boundaries.

We felt very fortunate to have been sent to Kyoto, and began setting up our message center on the sixth floor of a modern 12-story building downtown. Our living quarters were in a converted office building a few blocks away. We still slept on our fold-up army cots, but finally we were indoors for a change. With the exception of one night in an old hotel on Magnetic Island off the coast of Townsville, Australia, this was the first time any of us had slept indoors for the past three years! Imagine sleeping in a tent or out in a field every night for that long. I still find it hard to believe.

Kyoto must have been our reward and a very nice one at that. The town was clean and neat and the young Japanese girls were oh so sweet. People went about their daily routine in a manner that made us feel that we were in an Allied town for long await- ed R&R. Could these be the same people we had been at war with the past four years? Are they the brothers and sisters of the men that killed thousands at Pearl Harbor? Truthfully, we were so glad that the war was over, we just wanted to be friends with everybody, and made great attempts to do just that.

I wanted to see all of Kyoto, or as much as possible in the time allotted to us. I visited the Buddhist temples, parks and even went into a bank. Since I had worked for the Peoples Bank in Charlottesville, I thought it would be interesting to visit one in Kyoto. The employees seemed a little uneasy when I first entered but I assured them that I meant no harm. I just wanted to tell my banker friends back home that I had visited a branch under the Rising Sun.

The Japanese women, at least the young women I had the plea- sure of meeting, were great. In the United States we have what is called a nightclub where mostly young people go to party. A place to gather with friends to gossip, tell jokes, dance and listen to good music. They have the same type of establishments in Japan as well. There, however, the men would go alone and pick out their com- panion for the evening when they arrived. A great deal for the American service men. We didn't know any Japanese women, so to be able to go into a large room filled with lovely ladies and choose your companion for the party was a dream come true.

There were about six or eight of us Americans roaming about the entertainment area of downtown Kyoto in an attempt to make plans for Saturday night. We finally located what we had heard was the finest club in town. As luck would have it, there were

General Walter Krueger, head of the 6th Army in South Pacific.
Photo taken by Tom Behrendt in Kyoto, Japan in 1945.

several dancing girls there also making plans for the night. There was some type of rule or law that required the dancing girls to register several hours ahead of time in order to be eligible. We were told there would be a large crowd in attendance that evening, so I quickly picked one of the girls we had just met to be my dancing partner for the evening. These girls didn't speak a word of English so we had to use sign language, and the young lady indicated that she would be waiting.

There were some married Japanese men in attendance along with the Americans and apparently it was one of their customs to leave the wife at home when the husband went out to a club. Not a great deal for the Japanese housewife. In any case, these girls were not Geisha's, they were simply known as dancing girls. A Geisha was different in that she lived with a man when he traveled on business.

Since we didn't want to spend the evening drinking sake (Japanese wine), two of our guys went to a local brewery and bought six cases of Japanese beer and brought it back to the club. We put five tables together and were ready for the party.

We returned to the company headquarters at the message center. We had our customary army chow, shined our shoes (an important duty in the Army), took showers, put on clean uniforms and all together headed back to our newfound pleasure palace in downtown Kyoto.

We were filled with great anticipation of things to come. One of my buddies said "This is the way a war should end – in fact, this is the way all wars should end!" Another G.I. chimed in, "Too bad we couldn't have had basic training and then come directly here to Kyoto and eliminated the past four years!" (Well, there were many reasons for what had happened and what we had to do. Besides, what would I have written about?) That old cliché, "All's well that ends well" certainly applied to our situation.

We finally got back to the club and met up with the girls waiting for us. We went to our tables with our cases of beer, sat down and waited for the band to begin playing. After only a few minutes of getting acquainted, about a dozen or so middle aged Japanese men appeared on the bandstand with instruments in hand. They took their places in straight back chairs behind the familiar sheet-music stands and placed their music arrangements in the pre-determined order. (We really didn't know what to expect. We had heard Japanese music before and wondered how on earth we would be able to dance to that!) The leader stood in front of the band with the downbeat and out came non other than "In the mood" by Glenn Miller, "Sunny Side of the Street" by Tommy Dorsey, Woodchopper's Ball" by Woody Herman. It went on and on, one big band hit after another. We couldn't believe what we were hearing. We would never have imagined a Big Band of middle-aged Japanese men in a club in Kyoto, Japan playing the current popular music of the United States. After all, this was 1945 and the war had just ended, but these men played those tunes as if they had written each one themselves. The music quality was superb and done in the exact arrangement and style of the original orchestra in the U.S. The American soldiers stood in happy awe and we all showed our appreciation by dancing all night.

The Japanese had lost the war and that night they certainly treated us as the conquering hero's! They impressed us as being one hell of a country.

A war between any two nations is unthinkable. As I look back on those four years of my life, I often wonder what it was all about, what it accomplished. We made great allies with those that were our enemies, and it gave us the opportunity to meet and become friends with our allies throughout the world.

I am so happy that I had the chance to live in Australia for a year and then a year or so later while in New Guinea to earn a leave to return to Australia, this time to Sidney for a month. I don't want to completely ignore New Guinea because I did spend a year of my life on that God-for-saken, snake-ridden island. Leyte in the Philippines was definitely a step up from New Guinea, and then Manila was just a different world altogether. I would certainly never have traveled to Japan had it not been for the war, but it was a hell of a price to pay for my tour half way around the world. I thank God every day for providing the opportunity to make the trip there and back.

Three of my Message Center friends in Kyoto, Japan.

We made new friends in Kyoto. Making plans for the big party later that night.

*At a famous night club in Kyoto, Japan, October 1945. This lucky young thing
was my date!*

Making preparations for the big party in Kyoto in 1945.
Photo taken a few weeks after the Japanese surrendered.

京都 四條 大橋
THE SHIJO O-HASHI KYOTO

大阪字治ゆき

Kyoto, Japan

These girls were not beauty contest winners. Not even runner-ups! But, they did win for being the best dressed!

Standing from the left: Terry Hamlett, then Terry's daughter Andy Kraft, then Susan Gibson. Behind Susan is her son Lee Gibson; then JoAnne Kice. Behind JoAnne is Susan's husband (and Lee's father) "J.W." Gibson. Behind J.W. is Jimmy Hamlet holding his grandson. He's Terry's husband and Andy's father. Standing on the far right is Doris Behrendt, mother and grandmother; and wife of the author. Seated in front on left is Tracy Kraft, husband of Andy and next in front is Vinnie Kice, husband of JoAnne. Photo taken in 1999.

*Tom and Doris Behrendt at the Augusta Military Academy Reunion,
Fort Defiance, Virginia, 1994.*

"General" and Mrs. Thomas M. Behrendt of Charlottesville, VA.
(Photo taken in Atlantic City, NJ)

The Daily Progress

Lifestyle

Charlottesville, Virginia

December 31st, 1999

Behrendts celebrate 50th anniversary

Married New Year's Eve...50 Years Ago.

Mr. and Mrs. Thomas M. Behrendt were married in Charlottesville on December 31, 1949.

Their three daughters and their husbands, Terry and Jim Hamlett, Susan and J.W. Gibson, and JoAnne and Vinny Kice; their first grand-daughter and her husband, Amy and Tracy Kraft, along with their grand-son, Lee Chandler Gibson, and their newest granddaughter, Susan Mary Kice, will all be together for a grand anniversary celebration.

Mr. and Mrs. Thomas M. Behrendt

JoAnne Kice, Terry Hamlett, Susan Gibson and Mama Doris
The Behrendt girls in 1995.

What about all the other men that got there but didn't make it back? What about the shortened lives of these young men and the extreme loss suffered by their families' back home. Is there an answer? I don't know what is gained by dwelling on the past, but we must learn something. Must we continue doing this every few years until the end of time? Wouldn't it be better if we all got together to work on compromises before a war? I'm not a politician (and too old to start now) but we should all get on the stick and help straighten out this world. It is much too precious and there are too many wonderful people. Think about it, we may not get many more opportunities.

THE END

U.S. Army Photo

The War Ends

MORE GOOD BOOKS FROM HONORIBUS PRESS

THIS IS YOUR ORDER FORM – JUST CLIP and MAIL

_____ VALLEY OF THE SHADOW – Ed. Y. Hall $4.95
The Vietnam War. A young army officer's combat tour as an Advisor with
the South Vietnamese Army. Introduction by Gen. William C. Westmoreland.
1966-67. ISBN 0-9622166-0-7

_____ FLYING WITH THE HELL'S ANGELS – $5.95
Samuel P. Fleming as told to Ed. Y. Hall.
Memoirs of an Eighth Air Force Navigator's 30 missions over Fortress Europe
with the 303rd Bombardment Group. 1943-1944. ISBN 0-9622166-1-5

_____ UNPUBLISHED ACTIVITIES OF WORLD WAR II – $16.95
Earl J. Roberts.
Frontline duty with the infantry in Europe during World War II with the
187th Infantry Regiment. 1944-1945. Hard Cover. ISBN 940553-00-7

_____ ESCAPE! – James E. Armstrong $19.95
Memoirs of a B-17 pilot shot down over France and his amazing
escape story and return to England. 384th Bombarbment Group,
Eighth Air Force, 1943-1944.
Soft Cover. ISBN 1-885354-08-8

_____ THE SEARCH FOR MIAs – $12.95
Garry L. Smith, Edited by Ed. Y. Hall.
Answers to the question of "What happened to our Vietnam War
unaccounted for POWs and MIAs?" Soft Cover. ISBN 0-9622166-3-1

_____ HARRIET QUIMBY – $16.95
AMERICA'S FIRST LADY OF THE AIR – Ed. Y. Hall.
The tragic life of America's first licensed woman pilot, and the first woman
to pilot an aircraft across the English Channel 1875-1912. Hard Cover.
ISBN 1-885354-03-7

_____ HARRIET QUIMBY – $4.95
AN ACTIVITY BOOK FOR CHILDREN
Anita P. Davis / Ed. Y. Hall.
A companion activity work book for children (ages 10-14) to the book
Harriet Quimby – America's First Lady of the Air.
Soft Cover. ISBN 0-9622166-3-8

_____ HARRIET QUIMBY – A BIOGRAPHY $10.95
FOR INTERMEDIATE READERS
Anita P. Davis / Ed. Y. Hall.
Harriet's tragic story and life written for intermediate readers.
(Ages 8-14)
Hard Cover. ISBN 1-885354-06-1 70 p. 43 Illustrations.

_____ PACIFIC DIARY – Thomas M. Behrendt $12.95
Memoirs of a US Army World War II Signal Corps soldier and his trek
through the pacific war from Australia to Japan. Soft Cover.
ISBN: 1-885354-09-6 112 p. 63 Illustrations.

(TURN PAGE FOR MORE GOOD BOOKS)

_____ AIR FORCE: Official Service Journal of the   *$22.95
US Army Air Forces – Captain B.W. Peterson, USMCR
The primary medium for the exchange of ideas and information among
air personnel worldwide during WWII. Contains six facsimile monthly
copies – January 1943 - June 1943. Soft Cover. ISBN 0-9631875-1-1

_____ THUNDERBOLT – Lt. Col. Robert S. Johnson $19.95
America's first Fighter Ace to top Captain Eddie Rickenbackers
WWI victory record of 26 enemy aircraft – 8th AF, WWII, E.T.O.,
56th Fighter Group 1943-1944. Soft Cover. ISBN 1-885354-05-3

_____ NINE DAYS IN UNION – $12.95
THE SEARCH FOR ALEX AND MICHAEL SMITH –
Gary Henderson.
Behind the scenes, award winning story with Henderson and *Herald-Journal*
photographer Mike Bonner during the nine day national search for
the missing Smith boys. Soft Cover. ISBN 1-885354-00-2

_____ PROJECT 19 – A MISSION MOST SECRET –   Soft Cover: $19.95
John W. Swancara   *Hard Cover: $29.95
Even before the U.S. entered World War II, there was a secret
U.S. operated Air Depot in Ethiopia to repair planes for the RAF
being used against Rommel. This is the history of that secret base.
304 pages, 190 photographs, index, and documents.
Soft Cover. ISBN 1-885354-04-5   Hard Cover. ISBN 1-885354-07-X

TO ORDER

Please check the space next to the book(s) you want, send this order form together with your
check or money order, include the price of the book(s) and add $2.50 for the first book and
$1.00 for each additional book (* *Large books require extra postage of $4.00 per book.*) for han-
dling and mailing to:

HONORIBUS PRESS
P.O. BOX 4872
SPARTANBURG, SC 29305

I have enclosed $ _____ Check _____ or money
order as payment in full. Please no COD's.

Name _____

Address _____

City _____

State _____ Zip _____

Please allow 1-2 weeks for delivery.